BUILDING BLOCKS OF BIOLOGY

REPRODUCTION AND DEVELOPMENT

Written by Jeff De La Rosa

Illustrated by Ruth Bennett

www.worldbook.com

Co-published by agreement between Shi Tu Hui and World Book, Inc.

Shi Tu Hui
Room 1807, Block 1,
#3 West Dawang Road
Chaoyang District, Beijing 100025
P.R. China

World Book, Inc.
180 North LaSalle Street
Suite 900
Chicago, Illinois 60601
USA

© 2026. All rights reserved. This volume may not be reproduced in whole or in part in any form without prior written permission from the publisher.

WORLD BOOK and the GLOBE DEVICE are registered trademarks or trademarks of World Book, Inc.

Library of Congress Control Number: 2025942741

Building Blocks of Biology
ISBN: 978-0-7166-6737-7 (set, hard cover)

Reproduction and Development
ISBN: 978-0-7166-6744-5 (hard cover)

Also available as:
ISBN: 978-0-7166-6764-3 (e-book)
ISBN: 978-0-7166-6754-4 (soft cover)

WORLD BOOK STAFF

Editorial

Vice President
Tom Evans

Senior Manager, New Content
Jeff De La Rosa

Proofreader
Nathalie Strassheim

Graphics and Design

Senior Visual Communications Designer
Melanie Bender

Acknowledgments
Writer: Jeff De La Rosa
Illustrator: Ruth Bennett/The Bright Agency

TABLE OF CONTENTS

A Visit to the Country 4
Reproduction 6
Sexual Reproduction 10
Plant Reproduction 16
Pollination 18
Asexual Reproduction 24
Science Fun with Root:
Sweet Potato Slips 26
Growth and Development 28
Metamorphosis 30
A Farmer Is Born 32
Life on the Edge: Cloning 34
Show What You Know 38
Answers and Words to Know 40

There is a glossary on page 40. Terms defined in the glossary are in type **that looks like this** on their first appearance.

So do those barn kittens...

And even those goslings!

Yes, all of these animals reproduce through **sexual reproduction**...

Sexual reproduction involves special sex cells, called **gametes**.

The father provides a gamete called the sperm...

...and the mother provides a gamete called the egg.

ASEXUAL REPRODUCTION

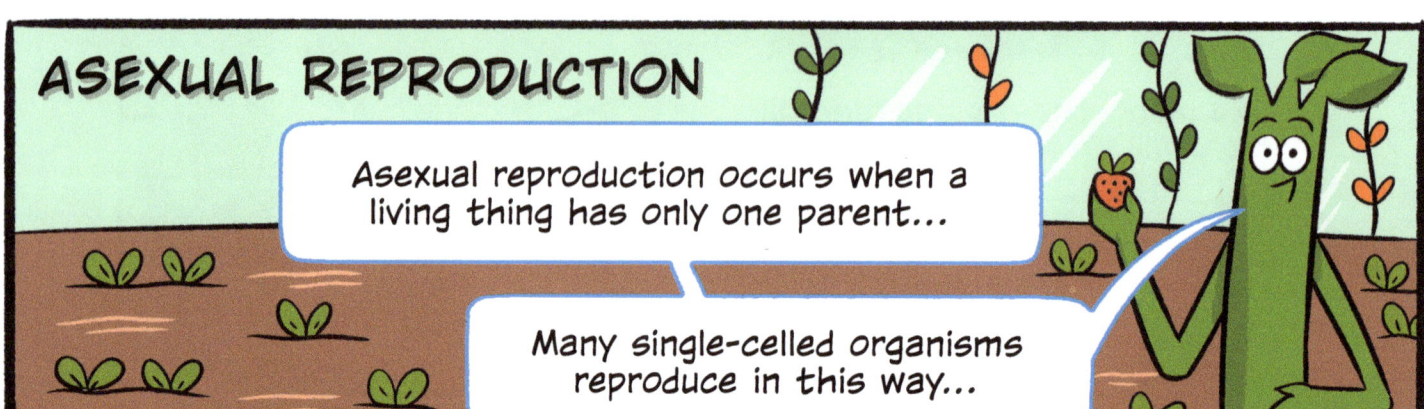

Asexual reproduction occurs when a living thing has only one parent...

Many single-celled organisms reproduce in this way...

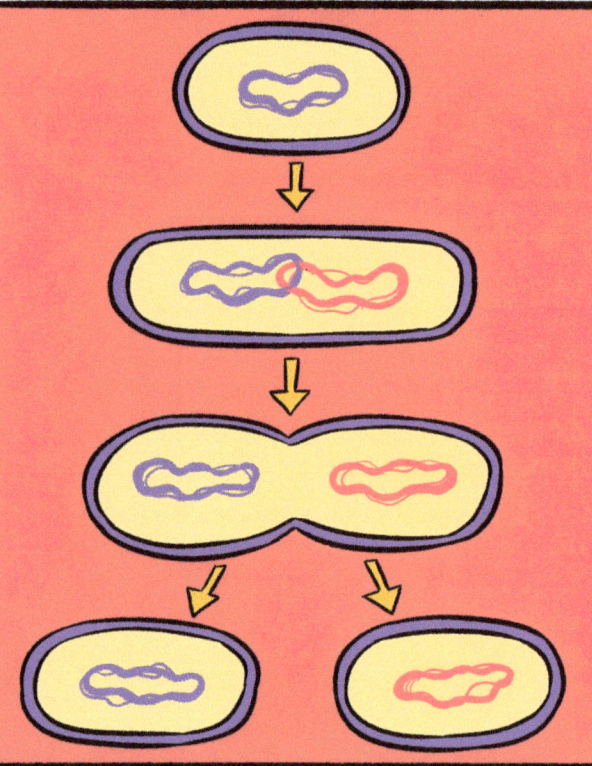

Bacteria, for example, simply divide in two, in a process called **binary fission.**

The result is two "offspring" bacteria, each with the same genes as the parent.

Some animals, such as sponges, use a type of asexual reproduction called **budding.**

A bud grows on the animal and eventually breaks off, forming a new organism.

SCIENCE FUN WITH ROOT

SWEET POTATO SLIPS

YOU WILL NEED:

- One large sweet potato
- A knife (Ask an adult for help!)
- Toothpicks
- Two cups big enough to fit the sweet potato halves
- Patience (Growing plants takes time!)

① Cut the sweet potato in half.

② Insert three or four toothpicks in each half as shown.

③ Place each half in a cup. Fill the cup with water until the bottom of the potato is submerged.

④ Place the cups on a sunny windowsill and wait. It may take a few weeks! Make sure to keep the water level above the bottom of the potato.

⑤ With luck, little leafy sprouts will grow. These sprouts are called slips, and they can be twisted off and planted to grow new sweet potatoes!

⑥ **Are slips an example of sexual or asexual reproduction? See page 40 for the answer.**

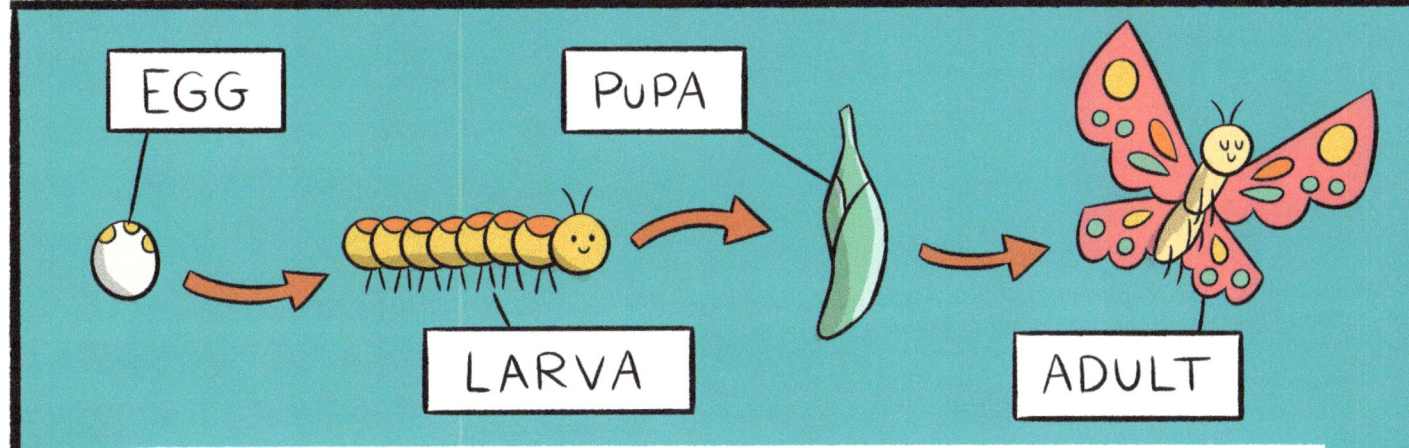

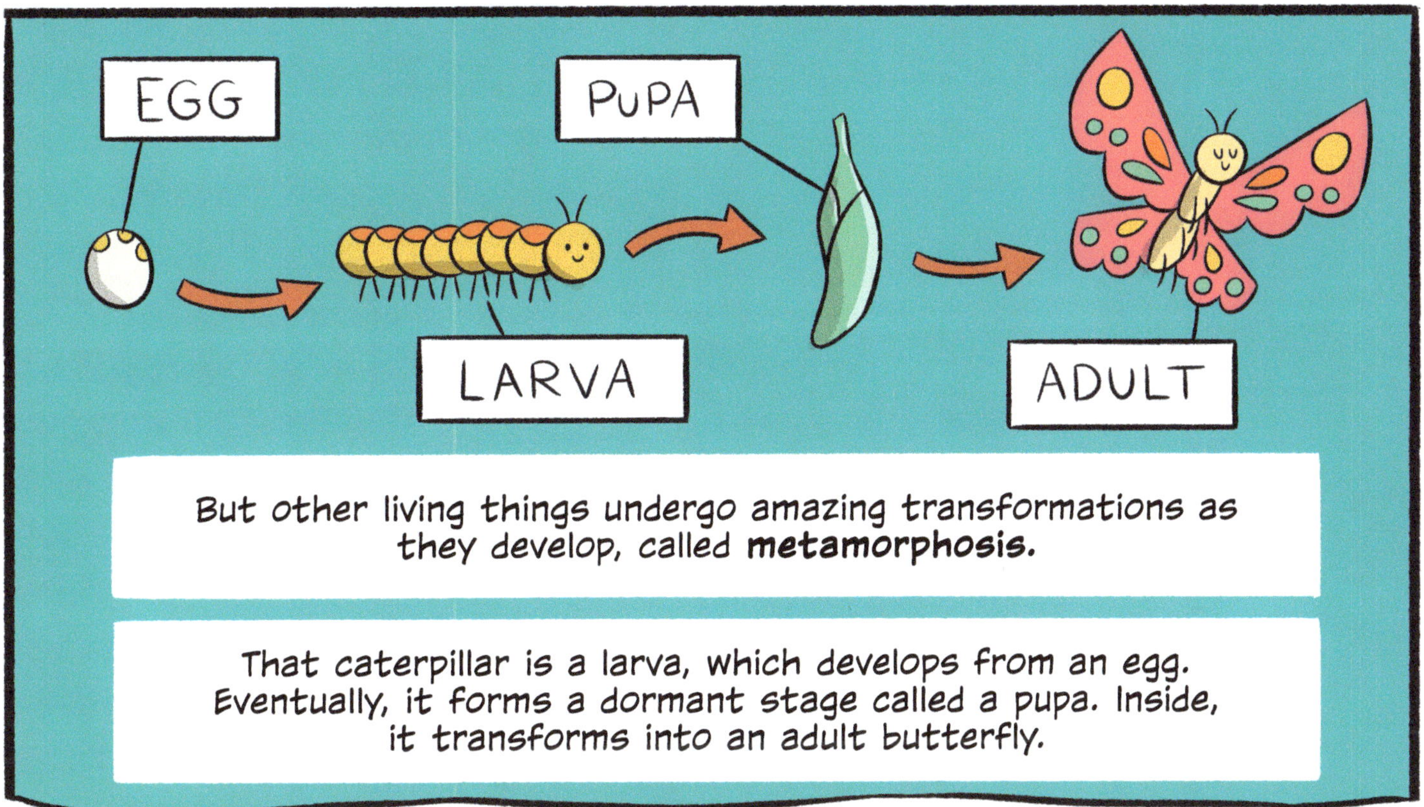

But other living things undergo amazing transformations as they develop, called **metamorphosis.**

That caterpillar is a larva, which develops from an egg. Eventually, it forms a dormant stage called a pupa. Inside, it transforms into an adult butterfly.

Frogs undergo metamorphosis, too!

Their eggs hatch into tiny tadpoles, which develop legs as they grow into adults.

Some animals undergo amazing transformations as they develop in a process called what? See page 40 for the answer.

LIFE on the EDGE
Ideas from the Cutting Edge of Biology
CLONING

A few weeks later...

Hey, Root! I've been thinking...

You showed us how to create identical copies of plants through vegetative propagation...

"No two living things are exactly alike...

Think of clones like identical twins, who share many traits but still aren't completely the same..."

Scientists clone animals by taking genetic material from an adult animal...

And transferring it into an egg cell, which can then grow into a new living thing.

SHOW WHAT YOU KNOW

1. True or false?

   A. All kinds of living things reproduce.
   B. In most mammals, fertilization happens outside the mother's body.
   C. All living things are exactly like their parents.
   D. Plants can reproduce sexually or asexually.

2. Is each of the following an example of sexual reproduction or asexual reproduction?

   A. a mother and father cat having kittens
   B. vegetative propagation
   C. pollination
   D. budding

3. Fill in the blanks.

Sexual reproduction involves special sex cells called _____ . The male cell is called _____ . The female cell is called the _____ . The two cells unite in a process called _____ .

4. What advantage does sexual reproduction have over asexual reproduction?

See page 40 for answers.

ANSWERS

page 15: gametes; fertilization

page 19: As bees visit flowers to feed on nectar, they can transfer pollen from stamen to pistil and flower to flower.

page 25: one parent; less diversity

page 27: asexual reproduction

page 31: metamorphosis

SHOW WHAT YOU KNOW ANSWERS pages 38-39:

1. A. true
   B. false
   C. false
   D. true

2. A. sexual reproduction
   B. asexual reproduction
   C. sexual reproduction
   D. asexual reproduction

3. gametes; sperm; egg; fertilization

4. Sexual reproduction produces greater diversity among offspring, which can help keep a species healthy.

WORDS TO KNOW

asexual reproduction reproduction involving only one parent.

binary fission reproducing asexually by dividing in two.

budding reproducing asexually through the growth of buds.

clones genetically identical organisms.

embryo a cluster of cells that grows from a fertilized egg.

fertilization the process by which male and female gametes combine.

gametes specialized male and female sex cells.

gene units of inheritance passed on from parents to offspring.

metamorphosis a dramatic transformation undergone by some species as they mature.

pollen tiny grains in plants that carry the male gametes.

reproduction the process by which living things make more of their kind.

sexual reproduction reproduction involving male and female sex cells.

vegetative propagation a form of asexual reproduction in plants.

www.ingramcontent.com/pod-product-compliance
Lightning Source LLC
Chambersburg PA
CBHW061257170426
43191CB00041B/2437